How to use this book

zop

Follow the advice, in italics, where given.
Support the children as they read the text that is shaded in cream.
***Praise** the children at every step!*
Detailed guidance is provided in the Read Write Inc. Phonics Handbook.
Activity 8 (Answer the 'questions to read and answer') only appears in Sets 4–7.

8 reading activities

Children:

1. *Practise reading the speed sounds.*
2. *Read the green and red words for the non-fiction text.*
3. *Listen as you read the introduction.*
4. *Discuss the vocabulary check with you.*
5. *Read the non-fiction text.*
6. *Re-read the non-fiction text and discuss the 'questions to talk about'.*
7. *Re-read the non-fiction text with fluency and expression.*
9. *Practise reading the speed words.*

Speed sounds

Consonants *Say the pure sounds (do not add 'uh').*

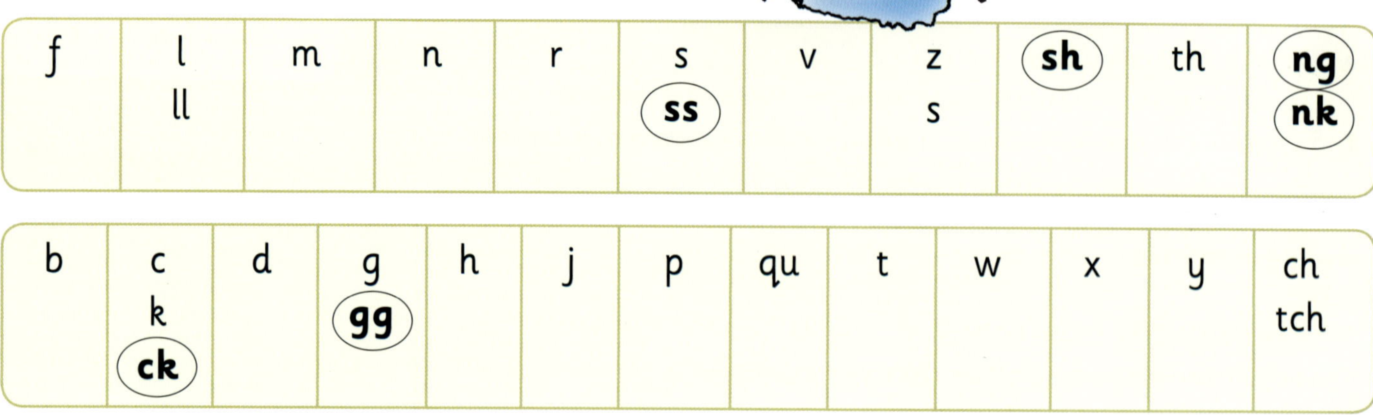

f	l ll	m	n	r	s **ss**	v	z s	**sh**	th	**ng** **nk**

b	c k **ck**	d	g **gg**	h	j	p	qu	t	w	x	y	ch tch

Vowels *Say the vowel sound and then the word, e.g. 'a', 'at'.*

at	hen	in	on	up	day	see	high	blow	zoo

*Each box contains one sound but sometimes more than one grapheme. Focus graphemes are **circled**.*

Green words

Read in Fred Talk (pure sounds).

went	tent	lamp	lunch	match	drank
Ed	grass	eggs	pond		

Read in syllables.

plas` tic → plastic    past` a → pasta   sal ` ad → salad

blank` et → blanket

Read the root word first and then with the ending.

twig → twigs		dish → dishes	
camp → camping		fish → fishing	

Red words

they the of to supper* for*

**red for this book only*

Camping

Introduction

Have you ever been on a camping trip?
Do you know how to put up a tent?
What else would you take to go camping?
In this book Ed and his dad go camping and have a lot of fun!

Written by Gill Munton

Vocabulary check

Discuss the meaning (as used in the non-fiction text) after the children have read the word.

	definition
plastic	*a hard, man-made material*
match	*a small, thin piece of wood with one end that makes fire*
supper	*an evening meal*

Punctuation to note:

Ed Dad	*Capital letters for names*
They Then	*Capital letters that start sentences*
.	*Full stop at the end of each sentence*
!	*Exclamation mark*
:	*Colon to show that a list is next*

Ed and Dad went camping.

They went in Dad's van.

Things for the camping trip:

- tent
- lamp
- blankets
- pans
- plastic cups and dishes
- things for lunch
- fishing rods

They put up the tent.

Then they sat on the grass.

They had eggs and pasta salad for lunch.

They drank cans of pop.

They went fishing in a pond. Ed got a big fish.

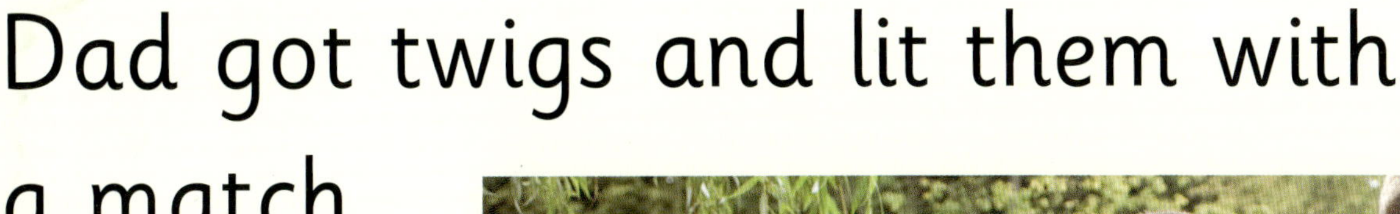

Dad got twigs and lit them with a match.

They had fish and salad for supper.

At ten o'clock they went to bed in the tent.

Ed and Dad had fun camping!

Questions to talk about

FIND IT

- ✓ *Turn to the page*
- ✓ *Read the question*
- ✓ *Find the answer*

Page 10:	*What did Ed and Dad bring to cook food in?*
Page 13:	*What did they have for lunch?*
Page 15:	*What did Dad use to make a fire?*
Page 16:	*What time did they go to bed?*

Speed words

Children practise reading the words across the rows, down the columns and in and out of order clearly and quickly.

went	eggs	lamp	and	bed
tent	fun	of	cup	twig
them	pan	on	pond	fish
in	dish	had	up	with